**This book is to be returned on or before
the last date stamped below.**

LIBREX

weblinks

You don't need a computer to use this book. But, for readers who do have access to the Internet, the book provides links to recommended websites which offer additional information and resources on the subject.

You will find weblinks boxes like this on some pages of the book.

weblinks

For more information on bullying, go to www.waylinks.co.uk/series/21debates/violence

waylinks.co.uk

To help you find the recommended websites easily and quickly, weblinks are provided on our own website, **waylinks.co.uk.** These take you straight to the relevant websites and save you typing in the Internet address yourself.

Internet safety

↗ Never give out personal details, which include: your name, address, school, telephone number, email address, password and mobile number.

↗ Do not respond to messages which make you feel uncomfortable – tell an adult.

↗ Do not arrange to meet in person someone you have met on the Internet.

↗ Never send your picture or anything else to an online friend without a parent's or teacher's permission.

↗ If you see anything that worries you, tell an adult.

A note to adults
Internet use by children should be supervised. We recommend that you install filtering software which blocks unsuitable material.

Website content

The weblinks for this book are checked and updated regularly. However, because of the nature of the Internet, the content of a website may change at any time, or a website may close down without notice. While the Publishers regret any inconvenience this may cause readers, they cannot be responsible for the content of any website other than their own.

HODDER
Wayland

21ST
CENTURY
DEBATES

VIOLENCE
IN SOCIETY
THE IMPACT ON OUR LIVES

RONDA ARMITAGE

HODDER
Wayland

an imprint of Hodder Children's Books

21st Century Debates Series

Genetics • Surveillance • Internet • Media • Artificial Intelligence • Climate Change • Energy • Rainforests • Waste, Recycling and Reuse • Endangered Species • Air Pollution • An Overcrowded World? • Food Supply • Water Supply • World Health • Global Debt • Terrorism • The Drugs Trade • New Religious Movements • Racism • Tourism • Globalisation • Transportation

Produced for Hodder Wayland by White-Thomson Publishing Ltd, 2/3 St Andrew's Place, Lewes, East Sussex BN7 1UP

© 2003 White-Thomson Publishing Ltd

Published in Great Britain in 2003 by Hodder Wayland, an imprint of Hodder Children's Books.

Project editor: Kelly Davis
Commissioning editor: Steve White-Thomson
Proofreader: David C. Sills, Proof Positive Reading Service
Series and book design: Chris Halls, Mind's Eye Design
Picture research: Shelley Noronha, Glass Onion Pictures

British Library Cataloguing in Publication Data
Armitage, Ronda
    Violence in society. - (21st Century Debates)
    1. Violence - Juvenile literature
    I. Title
    303.6
ISBN 0 7502 4210 8

Printed in Hong Kong by Wing King Tong Co. Ltd.

Hodder Children's Books, a division of Hodder Headline Limited, 338 Euston Road, London NW1 3BH

Picture acknowledgements: Camera Press 43; Howard Davies/Exile Images 8, 15, 32, 44, 58 and cover background; HWPL 40; Impact Photos 23 (Peter Arkell); Popperfoto 5, 7 above (Yannis Behrakis), 7 below and 26 (Corinne Dufka), 12, 27 (David van der Veen), 28 (Saeed Khan), 35, 37, 41, 42, 47 (Aditia), 48 (Gil Cohen Magen), 53 and cover foreground (Philippe Laurenson), 54 (Steve Marcus), 55 (Emilio Morenatti), 57; Rex Features 29 (Denis Cameron), 30, 34 (A. Krause), 46; Topham 4, 10 and 36 (Bob Daemmrich/The Image Works), 12, 13 (Eastcott/Momatiuk/The Image Works), 16, 17, 19 (Peter Hvizdak/The Image Works), 20, 21, 25, 33, 39, 50, 52.

Cover: foreground picture shows British football fans clashing with French youths in Marseilles in 1998; background picture shows weapons confiscated in Cambodia.

Every effort has been made to trace copyright holders. However, the publishers apologise for any unintentional omissions and would be pleased in such cases to add an acknowledgement in any future editions.

CONTENTS

A Violent World 4

Family Violence 10

Violence in Young People's Lives 22

Violent Crime 30

Racism and Violence 40

Political Violence 46

Violence as Entertainment 50

Preventing Violence 56

Glossary 60

Books to Read 62

Useful Addresses 62

Index 63

A VIOLENT WORLD

Violent by nature?

From ancient times the world has been a violent place where many people have had to fight to survive. But human beings are unique as a species, in that we will fight and kill even when our survival does not depend on it. We will use violence to gain dominance over other individuals, groups or nations for personal, racial, religious or economic advantage.

Violence is a part of all our lives. Some of us have been victims of violence ourselves, or know someone who has. In addition, television, radio and newspaper reports of wars, murders, rapes and child abuse make us all aware of the violence that exists in the world. This violence in society affects all of us in one way or another, from being careful about going out at night to parents worrying about children travelling on their own to school.

It is difficult to know whether violence in all its forms is more common today than it used to be. The keeping of crime statistics is a relatively recent activity; figures are not available for violence in, say, fourteenth-century Europe. However, we like to think of ourselves as more civilized than our ancestors so most of us find violent behaviour extremely shocking and offensive. Certainly there

Violence has always been part of humankind's struggle to survive. This artist's impression shows our prehistoric ancestors, about 20,000 years ago, trapping a woolly mammoth in a specially dug pit, and killing it with stone weapons.

is a widespread belief, even among people with a fairly high standard of living, that crime, particularly violent crime, is on the increase.

Defining violence

'Violence: physically aggressive behaviours that do, or potentially could, cause injury or death.' Although dictionary definitions of violence vary, most emphasize the physical aspects of the act. But it is possible to define violence more broadly than this. For instance, violence can be psychological: a person may be mentally damaged by repeated cruelty or threats. Sexual abuse and rape also usually involve coercion (forcing someone to do something they don't want to do, often in order to avoid further harm). Children and adults exposed to all sorts of violent situations, such as long-term family violence or war, sometimes suffer from post traumatic stress disorder which can affect both their physical and mental health for long periods of time.

Terrified Roman Catholic children are shielded by parents and police officers during violent protests as they make their way to Holy Cross Primary School in North Belfast in September 2001.

What makes people violent?

All of us have sometimes become angry or seen others in a violent mood. We may feel aggressive but our violence remains a feeling, it does not result in violent behaviour.

So why are some individuals more aggressive, and why do they actually commit violent acts? Explanations have varied over time. For example, in the nineteenth century the Italian psychiatrist Cesare Lombroso suggested that people inherited the criminal gene. In other words, he believed it was nothing to do with their upbringing or experience of life – criminals were born, not made. Later it was thought that certain inherited psychological traits, such as dishonesty or the inability to meet other people's needs, made individuals more likely to turn to crime and violence. Over the twentieth century, these ideas were replaced by theories emphasizing the role of social factors such as poverty, inequality and family upbringing, and crime statistics seem to support these theories. For instance, in prosperous, democratic countries, such as Sweden, Norway and Japan, with a relatively small gap between rich and poor, and little social inequality in terms of class, there is relatively less crime.

Violence in war

War is the most devastating violence that human beings wreak upon each other. The twentieth century, with two world wars, saw more humans killing other humans than all previous centuries combined. All weapons of war are designed to kill but twentieth-century advances in science and technology have generated new kinds of warfare that enable the greatest amount of damage to be done from the farthest distance. Much of the fighting against terrorists in Afghanistan in 2001, for instance, was conducted from the air, using bombs and missiles to search out enemy targets.

Major weapons of mass destruction, such as nuclear bombs, destroy all life and property for miles around and leave the area contaminated with radiation for years to come.

However the vast majority of wars during recent years have been civil wars. These wars have not only caused millions of deaths but also triggered a worldwide refugee crisis, as people have left their villages and countries to escape the fighting.

A US Air Force B-52 carpet bombs the Taliban positions north-west of Kabul, Afghanistan, in October 2001. The B-52s pounded the hardline Islamic movement in some of the heaviest strikes of the campaign.

A survivor of a massacre of Tutsi refugees, holding her two children, in a temporary camp which has been set up to protect them. Over 270 civilians were killed during the attack on the Tutsi refugee camp in north-west Rwanda. The killings were carried out by Hutu militias during the civil war in Rwanda, in 1994.

FACT

In 1997, the world's 225 richest people had a combined wealth of over $1,000 billion. Only 4 per cent of this wealth, $40 billion, would be enough to pay for basic education and healthcare, adequate food and safe water and sanitation for all.

Ethnic differences and poverty have been major factors in many civil wars. Political stability is largely dependent on economic stability so the poorer the country, and the more deprived large sections of its population, the greater the likelihood of large-scale unrest. Of the world's most indebted countries, twelve have suffered civil war or violent conflict in the last few decades. These countries are: Angola, Central African Republic, Comoros, Democratic Republic of the Congo, Ethiopia, Guinea-Bissau, Liberia, Sierra Leone, Somalia, Sudan, and Uganda and Mozambique (both now recovering from conflict).

Weapons confiscated by police in Cambodia. Many Cambodians have weapons, particularly guns, from the long years of war.

Is violence ever acceptable?

Whatever the dictionary says, in practice we may or may not describe certain acts as criminal or violent depending on our culture and the circumstances or period of history in which they occur. For example, during wars, all manner of brutalities, that at any other time would be regarded as 'cold-blooded murder', are seen as both acceptable and necessary.

Even in everyday life there sometimes seems to be little logic in the way society deals with different forms of violence. Sweden, among other countries, has banned all corporal punishment of children. Meanwhile in the UK, and the US, parents are still permitted to smack children. Yet if the same people smacked an adult they could be charged with assault. And, throughout the world, police and the legal system view domestic violence less seriously than violence by a stranger.

Furthermore, violence can be psychological as well as physical. For instance, workplace bullying (the abuse of power by a person in authority, such as an employer) is becoming an increasing problem. Workplace bullying has been described as offensive treatment through vindictive, cruel or humiliating attempts to undermine an individual or group of employees. It occasionally takes the form of physical harassment but more often constant destructive criticism, humiliating personal remarks in front of colleagues, spreading gossip and starting rumours.

Is violence inevitable?

There are some examples of non-violent societies. For instance, the Hutterites, a religious sect living in Canada and the USA, in a classless society where economic resources were shared fairly equally, had no murders and only one suicide in 100 years of settlement (1874-1974). Samoa, an island in the Pacific, also has very little crime, perhaps partly due to Samoans' strong sense of loyalty to their family, community and church. In addition, very few Samoans experience poverty, and resources are usually shared equally.

FACT

During the First World War, hundreds of British soldiers were killed by their own troops for refusing to engage in killing the enemy.

weblinks

For more information on children and poverty go to www.waylinks.co.uk/series/21debates/violence

DEBATE

How would you define violence? Think about your own life and consider if and when you have ever experienced any violence.

FAMILY
VIOLENCE

Happy families?

Most people throughout the world live at least part of their lives in a family group. Or it may be an extended family, made up of grandparents, aunts, uncles and cousins as well as parents and children. However, for an increasing majority, the family means a nuclear family – one or two parents or step-parents and their children living in a family home. Whatever the situation, the hope is that the adults will be happy and the children will be raised in a loving environment. However the evidence suggests that there are a great many unhappy families.

Some families, like these Vietnamese parents and their children living in Texas, USA, enjoy life together, while other families are torn apart by conflict and violence.

Murder, assault and sexual abuse are all more likely to be carried out by a member of the victim's family than by anyone else. Family violence (often known as domestic or private violence) is common throughout the world. And research shows that, although women and young children are most likely to be the victims, it can happen to any family member.

Family life involves more emotional intensity and personal intimacy than most other human relationships. Because family ties are often charged with strong, contradictory emotions, including both love and hate, a quarrel that breaks out in the home can spiral out of control more quickly than it would in another social setting, where the participants would have to modify their behaviour because they were with other people. Family violence happens behind closed doors.

Children and family violence
The National Society for the Prevention of Cruelty to Children (NSPCC) defines child cruelty as '…Neglect, physical injury, sexual or emotional abuse inflicted or knowingly not prevented, which causes significant harm or death.' While sexual abuse is disapproved of in all cultures, definitions of 'neglect', 'physical injury' and 'emotional abuse' vary from culture to culture, and there are widely differing ideas on how children should be brought up. For instance, in some Indian families there is an emphasis on corporal punishment but this is seen as an expression of parental concern rather than hostility to the child. Likewise, traditional Chinese culture emphasizes the principle of filial devotion (or *xiao*). Children are expected to be absolutely obedient to their parents. In extreme cases this could even mean the child sacrificing his or her own life for the sake of the parents.

VIEWPOINT

'Our society fails to give children their real value. Children are often seen as objects to exploit, not individuals, so their needs aren't given the priority they deserve.'
NSPCC, Full Stop Campaign, 2000

VIEWPOINTS

'Considering that previous research shows that anti-social behaviour in childhood is associated with violence and other crime as an adult, society as a whole, not just children, could benefit from ending the system of child rearing that goes under the euphemism [name] of spanking.'
University of New Hampshire, US, 1998

'We are not talking about beating them up, but a little slap doesn't do them any harm.'
Dr George Carey, Archbishop of Canterbury, UK, 1998

In Victorian Britain the children of the poor, particularly orphans, often experienced extreme hardship and abuse. These homeless boys were photographed in around 1880, when they were admitted to a children's home run by a charity.

Who are the abusers?

For many children some form of violence is a part of their everyday lives because their abuser is another family member. In the UK, since 1970, between five and seven children a year have been killed by a stranger, while in 2002 it was estimated that one to two children each week were killed by their parents or carers. Mothers are just as likely as fathers to harm their children physically. The only violent crime where women exceed men is physical cruelty to children under four years – perhaps because women are usually still the main carers of young children and babies and therefore spend more time with them.

However, child sexual abuse by women is rare; men are the main abusers. There are many reasons why some adults take advantage of their authority over young people. Social factors, such as poverty and unemployment, create considerable stress for families who may be isolated within their community, without extended family or friends. The feeling of having no power within adult relationships, or having been abused as a child, may also play a part. Most adults who harm children experienced destructive childhoods themselves.

Protecting children

Countries in the developed world have laws to protect children from being harmed by adults. In the UK, various acts (including the Children Act, passed in 1989) grant power to Social Services, the police and the NSPCC to intervene to protect children at risk. In the most serious cases of harm, children will be placed on the Child Protection Register or will be taken into care. In 1998, it was estimated that there were 200,000 children living away from home, either in residential institutions or in foster care. The Children Act also shifted the emphasis from parent's rights over a child to their duties and responsibilities towards the child.

Women as victims of violence

In 1981, the anthropologist David Levinson reported that the most common form of family violence throughout the world was wife beating. Until the nineteenth century, women in most societies were seen as being owned by their husbands and therefore of lower status. Physical punishment was often used to keep women under control. A married woman's body, her property, her earnings and her children all belonged to her husband to do with as he wished.

FACT

In the UK, three out of four children who have been in long-term care (in children's homes or living with foster families) have no academic qualifications or employment when they leave their care homes or foster families. A third of young homeless people have been in care; and 40 per cent of the young people in prison have been in care.

A young woman waits to be admitted to a domestic violence shelter.

VIEWPOINT

'...a wife batterer ... has learned that striking out against another relieves stress, helps him to feel powerful, masculine and in control. This coping mechanism is extremely destructive and hurtful to others.'
Dr Paul Hanck. Calm Down. 1980

Although various laws passed over the last 150 years have changed the position of women in developed nations, the idea that they should obey and serve men still persists and, until relatively recently, the majority of crimes against women were not taken seriously. They were seen merely as domestic disputes that occurred as a normal, acceptable part of any relationship.

Then, in 1994, the United States Congress passed the Violence Against Women Act. Three million dollars were set aside to re-establish a national helpline for victims and survivors of domestic abuse. The police were given better training in order to understand the issues involved in family violence and more legal protection was provided for battered women. Similar laws and services have been established throughout Europe, New Zealand and Australia.

Despite these developments, it has been estimated that, in the UK, US, Australia and New Zealand, one in four women lives in a violent relationship. Some 80 per cent of all women murdered know their killer. The biggest single category of killer is a husband, partner or ex-partner. Until 1991, rape within marriage was not recognized in Britain. The House of Lords then ruled that a husband has no right to force himself on his wife. During the 1990s, there was an increase in the number of reported incidents where the victim knew the rapist. Relatives, friends, former partners or recent aquaintances commit some 43 per cent of sexual assaults. A considerable proportion of violent crime in Europe and the US is domestic violence, rather than violence at the hands of a stranger.

Women around the world
However, change has taken place more slowly in other parts of the world. In developing regions,

VIEWPOINTS

'Statistics reveal that 30 per cent of women are regularly beaten by their husbands.'
The Ministry of Social Affairs. Egypt. 2002

'So what? A woman's role is to obey her husband; if she does not then she deserves what she gets.'
Cab driver. Cairo. Egypt. 2002

such as Africa and Asia, women often have lower status than men. Fewer educational and job opportunities are available to them so they remain more dependent on fathers or husbands for support. In 1990, Iraq passed an official order allowing men to kill their wives for adultery even if it was unproven.

India has a particular problem with dowry-related violence. If a newly married woman's husband is dissatisfied with the dowry (usually money or goods) provided by her family on their wedding, she may be burned alive. Although dowries are now illegal in India, they are still common in rural areas. According to the Indian government, sixteen Indian women are killed in dowry burnings each day.

FACT

Violence by male partners is the single largest cause of injury to women worldwide – more than muggings and car accidents combined.

weblinks

For more information on violence against women go to
www.waylinks.co.uk/series/ 21debates/violence

Domestic violence awareness poster, Cambodia, 2001. It is estimated that one in six Cambodian women are physically abused by their husbands.

FACT

About one-third of women murdered in both Japan and the US each year are killed by their husbands.

Primary school boys often play roughly at breaktime, whereas girls tend to spend more time talking. Are boys naturally more aggressive or are they influenced by society's expectations of men?

A 1992 report from Brazil noted that wife-murder is a common crime, and that men who commit wife-murder are often found 'not guilty' because it is still acceptable to defend a man's honour by means of murder. For example, many Brazilians believe that a husband is perfectly right to execute an unfaithful wife. The courts would see this as an act of self-defence. And, because women are considered to belong to men, any attempt they make to protect themselves is seen as a threat to their husbands.

Men who batter

Men who abuse come from all walks of life, all classes, all races and all ages. Some are violent only to their partners, not to anyone else. But over half those men who are violent to their partners also abuse their children. Some research suggests that the causes are social. From an early age it is considered more acceptable for boys to resolve issues by fighting. 'Tough guy' images in film and video may also contribute to the view men develop of themselves. Many will have learned violent behaviour as children, either by being abused or humiliated or by witnessing violence being used as a way of resolving conflict in their families. As adults, they often associate with men who have similar outlooks and so continue to believe that such behaviour is right. Men who feel powerless within a relationship may use violence as a means of trying to demonstrate power and control.

Women and family violence

At the same time, men are increasingly becoming the victims of domestic violence. Those most likely to be attacked are in their early thirties, unmarried, but living with a woman. A British Crime Survey, carried out in 1999, showed that there were over 6 million assaults in the home each year, almost evenly split between men and women perpetrators. But male violence to women is much more likely to result in death, physical injury and lasting harm than women's violent acts to men.

Parent abuse

Parents have a position of power and authority in a family, and – within certain limits – it is assumed that they will decide how that power is used. Society shows considerable disapproval of children who are violent to their parents, yet parents are often blamed for their children's violent behaviour.

Junior members of Umkhonto We Sizwe (the militant wing of the African National Congress) demonstrate their fighting skills at a 1993 rally in Soweto, South Africa.

FACT

During the Vietnam War, 58,000 American soldiers were killed. During the same period, between 30,000 and 54,000 American women were killed in their homes.

The jury in the trial of Lyle (right) and Erik Menendez, accused of murdering their wealthy Beverly Hills parents, found them guilty on both counts of murder even though they claimed to have been abused by their parents.

Research shows that older children and young adults do inflict injuries on their parents in considerable numbers. For instance, in the USA about 10 per cent of parents with a ten- to seventeen-year-old living at home will experience at least one violent act a year. Over 3 per cent of these adolescents were reported to have kicked, punched, beaten up or used a gun or knife against a parent. In extreme cases, children have killed a parent.

Elder abuse

Abuse of the elderly is on the increase. This is partly to do with numbers. In the developed world, better food, better healthcare and improved living conditions have all contributed to an increase in the elderly population. Although many elderly people may remain in their own homes until they die, others need to be cared for. The rising cost of care in institutions means that a growing number of elderly people become the responsibility of their families. This may place increasing pressures on their adult children, in terms of accommodation, finance or a restriction in lifestyles.

FACT

In 1994, in the seventy-five largest urban areas in the US, 2 per cent of all murder victims were parents killed by their children.

Abusive treatment of the elderly can take many forms. Carers may tie their elderly relatives to a bed while they go out shopping. Others may be bullied into changing a will or handing over house deeds to the carer. Some elderly people are physically attacked – injuries can be easily dismissed as an accident. All these types of abuse can sometimes go unnoticed because the elderly are often isolated from the community and may find it difficult to report abusive incidents.

Violence in gay and lesbian relationships

One of the most overlooked forms of family violence is that in gay and lesbian relationships. During the 1970s and 1980s, discussion of 'family violence' tended to focus solely on heterosexual relationships. The emphasis, too, was on domestic violence as something that men do to women. Prejudice about gay men and women stopped many victims of this form of family violence from speaking out. It was not until 1999 that legislation was passed in Britain ruling that a homosexual couple in a stable relationship could be defined as a family. Evidence now suggests that violence between homosexual couples is at least as great as that between heterosexual couples.

> **FACT**
>
> Only about 5 per cent of elder abuse complaints are made by the victims themselves. As with other forms of family violence, they assume they are somehow to blame for the abuse. Sometimes, as an elderly parent, they are embarrassed to admit they have raised a child who is capable of such behaviour. Often their love for the abuser is stronger than the desire to leave the abusive situation.

In developed countries people are living much longer than they used to, and the elderly can be very vulnerable to violence. This 99-year-old First World War veteran was photographed in 1998 with his 84-year-old wife in Meriden, Connecticut, USA.

VIEWPOINT

'We need to cancel the hitting license in society. The elimination of spanking as a child-rearing technique; gun control, to get deadly guns out of the home; elimination of corporal punishment in school; elimination of the death penalty; and an elimination of media violence that glorifies and legitimises violence. Reducing poverty, inequality, and unemployment and providing for adequate housing and medical care,... and providing educational opportunities are steps that could reduce stress in families.'
Richard Gelles, Intimate Violence in Families, *1997, USA*

Counting the cost

Studies show that children who are abused live in constant fear, feeling powerless to take any action to stop the violence and abuse. Parents are unable to meet their children's needs and the children may become either increasingly withdrawn or more aggressive. In the long term, some of these children will find it difficult to trust people and form lasting relationships.

On average, women in the UK will suffer an abusive relationship for six years before asking for help. The stress of living in these conditions can trigger a range of physical and mental illnesses in victims of family violence. These include depression, anxiety, eating problems and post traumatic stress disorder.

The cost to society

It is very difficult to calculate the financial costs of family violence. There are medical and therapy bills for physical and emotional damage; prison costs for those convicted; the costs of running safe refuges for battered women; housing costs after separation and divorce, social services, police and court costs; the list goes on. However, some estimates have been made. Violence against women is estimated to cost the US economy as much as $67 billion annually, based on the costs of medical treatment, lost worker productivity and quality of life. And in 1999, UK government agencies and charities spent around £1 billion on child abuse. Most of this money was spent on the consequences of abuse rather than its prevention.

A mother and her child find safety at a shelter for battered women in Tel Aviv, Israel.

Breaking the cycle

It is now widely recognized that violence and abuse are often part of a cycle of learned behaviour. A person who has experienced violence, particularly

A counselling session at a battered women's shelter in Texas, USA.

during early childhood, is more likely to become violent themselves, either to their spouse or children or both. Fortunately, fewer than half those whose childhoods were violent continue the cycle, and there are a number of initiatives to prevent abused children from becoming abusive parents. For example, in Ontario, Canada, doctors working with problem fourteen- to sixteen-year-olds advise them on how to get medical and social help. The participants assist in social work projects and use role play to work through their feelings. After several years, the doctors reported a three-fold decrease in violent behaviour.

DEBATE

How do you think family members should handle conflict in order to reduce the chances of violence in the home?

VIOLENCE IN YOUNG PEOPLE'S LIVES

The rights of children

In November 1989 the United Nations adopted the Convention on the Rights of the Child. This Convention changed the obligations of all adults to children everywhere. Most importantly, the 1989 Convention requires that children be safeguarded against all forms of abuse, neglect and exploitation. Nevertheless, in practice, even though there have been some improvements in child protection since the Convention was passed, children remain the most vulnerable and powerless group within all societies.

Homelessness

In the developed world, most child abuse and neglect takes place within families. In extreme circumstances these children will be removed to a safe place in order to ensure their survival. In recent years some have spent time in residential children's homes. Although many of these provide good standards of care, it has come to light that a few have been very abusive institutions that continued the cycle of abuse and violence.

Increasingly, in the developed world, many cities have large numbers of homeless people. Some young people, who have experienced abusive family situations or family breakdown, may either be forced to leave home or simply run away. The 'youth homelessness' problem includes young people living on the streets as well as on friends' floors or

FACT

Those who 'sleep rough' are four times as likely to be murdered as the general population. In the UK, the average life expectancy of rough sleepers is forty-two years (compared to the national average of seventy-four for men and seventy-nine for women).

— **weblinks**

For more information on
the rights of children
and young people go to
www.waylinks.co.uk/series/
21debates/violence

A homeless young man begging in a London street, 1989.

in hostels. Others have mental health problems or may have come to the city hoping to find employment. Once people find themselves without a permanent address, it becomes very difficult to find work and their lives may deteriorate into a spiral of deprivation and hardship.

Many homeless people of all ages become victims of crime, and some commit crimes in order to survive. Most view themselves as outsiders in society, excluded from the everyday activities, such as going to work, entertaining friends or keeping a bank account, that others take for granted.

Bullying

Most bullying takes place within schools but it can occur wherever groups of children gather together. Both males and females bully but their methods vary considerably. Boys tend to use name-calling and physical aggression, whereas girls are more likely to resort to 'psychological warfare' in order to control their victims, usually other girls. This 'girl-on-girl' cruelty, sometimes using text messaging on mobile phones, has spread through schools very rapidly.

VIEWPOINT

Descriptions of bullying by children and young people:
'**Being called names, being teased, being pushed or pulled about, being hit or attacked, having your bag or other possessions taken and thrown about, having rumours spread about you, being ignored and left out, being forced to hand over money or possessions, being attacked because of religion, race or colour.'**

FACT

After the 1999 massacre at Columbine High School, Colorado, USA, when Eric Harris and Dylan Klebold shot fifteen people and injured twenty-three more, it was revealed that the two killers had been subjected to repeated taunting, teasing, insults, name-calling, rejection and accusations (apparently false) of being homosexual.

FACT

In 1995 a little girl called Megan Kanka was raped and killed in the US. Nine months later Megan's Law was introduced. This allows communities access to names and addresses of known sex offenders who are required by law to give their addresses to the police. Opponents of this policy argue that it only drives paedophiles, fearful of persecution by the public, to go into hiding. This makes it harder for the authorities to keep track of their whereabouts.

Although most schools now take bullying seriously, a third of all girls and a quarter of boys in the UK in 2000 said they had been too afraid to go to school at some time in their lives. A report on the long-term effects of bullying found that adults who had been bullied as children experienced problems in later life, including low self-esteem, suicidal thoughts and difficulty relating to people. New ideas for making the bully accountable for his or her actions have been tried in many schools. In Washington State, USA, there is a school-based initiative called the Empower Programme, which enables both the bullies and the bullied to come together in a spirit of non-confrontational honesty and openness.

Violent children

In February 1993, two-year-old James Bulger was murdered in Liverpool. Two ten-year-old boys were convicted of his murder and people were appalled that young boys could have committed such a horrendous act. However, although little was heard about it at the trial, both boys had grown up in abusive households where they experienced neglect, bullying and physical violence. These factors may well have contributed to the boys' extremely violent behaviour. Despite the enormous media coverage of the Bulger case in Britain, murders by children are rare. A survey carried out in 1999 reported only seventeen murders by children under fourteen years old who had killed in Britain since the end of the Second World War.

Paedophiles and the Internet

This book, by its nature, focuses on violence, cruelty and abuse, but the fact is that most children grow up in a loving environment with parents who care for and protect them. However, growing public awareness of child abuse, particularly abuse by strangers, has frightened many parents and discouraged them from allowing children the freedom experienced in earlier generations.

Although most children who are sexually abused will know the person who abuses them, it is abuse by a stranger that arouses most fear. Paedophiles, who abduct and sexually abuse children, are seen as a particular threat. With the increased use of the Internet, some paedophiles have sought to get to know their victims through 'chatrooms', perhaps by posing as children or teenagers. For example, in 2000, a British paedophile was jailed for five years after he posed as a teenage boy and lured a thirteen-year-old girl to his home. The police and Internet providers continue to search for ways to trace suspected paedophiles.

weblinks

For more information on bullying go to www.waylinks.co.uk/series/21debates/violence

Mothers of murdered children lead a march through central London in 1996, demanding more action to protect youngsters from paedophiles.

FACT

In some countries, such as the Yemen and Colombia, it is cheaper to buy a gun than a book.

VIEWPOINT

'It is immoral that adults should want children to fight their wars. There is simply no excuse for arming children.'
Archbishop Desmond Tutu, South Africa

VIEWPOINT

'More children are able to become soldiers now because of new lightweight weapons which are easy for children to handle.'
Guardian newspaper, UK, 1999

Children and war

In many developing countries, children face different dangers. Some 600 million children are in families living on less than US$1 per day. According to the charity Save the Children, an estimated 300,000 children, some as young as seven, are fighting in wars or conflicts in countries such as Mozambique, Colombia, Afghanistan, Angola and Turkey. Most fighters are boys but girls are also used. Many girls are sexually abused and forced to be the 'wives' or unpaid servants of adult soldiers. Some children are kidnapped and made to fight. Others, who often come from very poor backgrounds or are refugees, join militias in order to get food and clothes and some way to defend themselves.

Child soldiers on an NPFL militia vehicle ride through the streets of Monrovia in 1996. Liberia's largest programme to rehabilitate child soldiers had its resources looted during the fighting and half the children chose to return to the streets and again take up arms.

These children are both perpetrators and victims of violence. Between 1985 and 1995, conflicts killed some 2 million children and injured 6 million others. Those who survive often have their childhoods stolen from them, and are left emotionally and physically devastated. The fall-out from war affects all members of society in the countries involved. War usually means that health services, and food and water supplies collapse. The resulting hunger and disease particularly affect the young and the elderly. People are often forced to flee their homes. Sometimes families are scattered, and the children may be lost, orphaned or abandoned.

Children and poverty

In the Indian sub-continent, and parts of Asia and Latin America, street children are a common sight. With conflicts in Eastern Europe, such as those in the former Yugoslavia, they are also appearing on the streets of European cities like Bucharest and Sarajevo. Some are orphans; others have been abandoned by families who are too poor or demoralized to look after them. They beg, they comb rubbish dumps for scraps, or work in restaurants earning only the food their employers give them. Some are forced into prostitution, others work as couriers for drug dealers. They are often victims of violence and frequently come into conflict with the police. They are sometimes treated as 'little more than vermin'. Most of these children have no chance of any education, which remains the best way out of poverty. More than 130 million of the world's children, most of them girls, do not even attend primary school.

weblinks

For more information on child soldiers go to www.waylinks.co.uk/series/ 21debates/violence

A ten-year-old Cambodian land mine victim tries out her new artificial leg, provided by a British charity, The Cambodia Trust. Cambodia is one of the most heavily mined countries in the world.

Child labour

Traditionally, children in developing countries often worked with their families, learning skills they would need as adults. But now, increasingly, children are forced to work for their own and their families' survival. They labour at exploitative, exhausting tasks in the fields, in makeshift factories, and in the households of the wealthy. Because of their age and more vulnerable position, employers find children easier to intimidate and cheaper to employ than adults. In India, children can earn between £60 and £75 per year, a significant amount for a family whose total annual income may be only £200.

A 14-year-old boy stitches footballs in his house in 1998, situated on the outskirts of Pakistan's major sporting goods manufacturing city Sialkot. The industry exports around 20 million footballs every year, but there are far fewer child labourers since the major exporters in Pakistan signed an agreement with the International Labour Organization in 1995.

In rural areas of Burkina Faso, children as young as five work to eat, many of them in unregulated goldmines where they are vulnerable to many dangers. They injure themselves with the heavy pick axes they have to use; and the 'galleries' where they work sometimes cave in. Usually they work in dirty conditions, without protection, so they are also vulnerable to diseases such as cholera. The International Labour Organization (ILO) estimates that, worldwide, some 250 million children under the age of fifteen work either full-time or part-time. And child labour is not restricted to developing countries. For instance, an estimated

Other children labour in factories, working long hours under harsh conditions, like these 'aluminium children' photographed in Cairo, Egypt, in 1998.

90,000 children aged between eight and fourteen work in the region around Naples in Italy. According to the United Nations Children's Fund (UNICEF), child labour flourishes because so many benefit from it, directly and indirectly:

- Employers exploit child workers and use their ready availability to force down adult wages.
- Governments benefit from increased exports and economic growth.
- Consumers at home and abroad enjoy lower prices of products.

Fortunately, there have been some successful attempts to limit or stop the use of child labour without removing the badly needed income that these children earn for their families. For instance, in 1995, UNICEF, the ILO and the Bangladesh Garment Manufacturers and Exporters Association agreed to end the practice in Bangladesh and release children from the factories where they worked to attend special local schools. These children are paid a regular allowance each month, contributed to by the three organizations, to make up for their lost wages.

weblinks

For more information on child labour go to www.waylinks.co.uk/series/21debates/violence

DEBATE

Imagine that you are drawing up your own Convention on the Rights of the Child. What do you think children's rights and responsibilities are? And how can people who are responsible for looking after children try to ensure that they are happy, healthy and safe?

VIOLENT CRIME

Throughout the world, murder is regarded as the most serious of crimes. It is also the easiest violent crime on which to get reliable statistics. Although murder cases receive a lot of coverage in the media, the global murder rate has gradually declined and is currently stable. At present, most people in developed countries have a far greater chance of being killed in a road accident than being murdered.

It is more difficult to assess the extent of other violent crimes, such as assault and rape. Research suggests that there has been a steady rise in violent crime since the Second World War. But during the twentieth century the public became increasingly aware of certain types of violence that had previously

Many women are frightened to walk alone at night because they believe they risk being violently assaulted or raped.

attracted little attention or were not unlawful. For example, women's groups encouraged the reporting of domestic violence and female rape, although male rape was not recognized in law until 1997.

In general, there has been a greater emphasis on crimes against the person (as opposed to crimes against property). Experts suggest that crime statistics may not be a reliable source for crime figures, as they only include crimes that are actually reported to the police. In the case of violent crime, it is thought that one-third of victims choose not to contact the police, claiming that it is a private affair.

Perpetrators of violent crime

The majority of violent criminals are young men who are likely to come from a background of poverty and live in inner cities. They are particularly connected with 'street crimes' such as theft, burglary, assault and rape, though the motivating factors behind each of these crimes is different. For example, rape of women is usually a violent expression of masculine power, dominance and toughness; whereas the growing problem of 'phone-jacking' (stealing mobile phones) probably has more to do with the increasing wealth of developed countries, where there are more valuables to steal.

Although statistics show that more women are getting involved in crime, their crimes (typically shoplifting, public drunkenness, drugs and prostitution) rarely involve violence. As for children, since the 1990s it appears that there has been an increase in some crimes of violence by children as young as ten. These are mostly boys but an increasing minority of girls get involved in committing certain violent offences. However, children are generally far more likely to be victims of violence than perpetrators.

VIEWPOINT

'"April, 29, 1994.
Dear Mr. Clinton,
I want you to stop the killing in the city. People is dead and I think that somebody might kill me. Would you please stop the people from deading. I'm asking you nicely to stop it. Do it now. I know you can.
Your friend
James."
While walking home from a picnic with his family, James Darby, 9 years old, was brutally and senselessly gunned down in a drive-by shooting 9 days after writing this letter to President Clinton.'
Joy D. Osofsky [ed.], Children in a Violent Society, 1997

FACT

In England and Wales, between 1992 and 2000, the number of ten- to seventeen-year-olds cautioned or convicted of an offence fell by about a third.

Media commentators often claim that there is a 'moral breakdown' among young people, pointing to the incidence of vandalism, school truancy and drug use in support of their case. However, some criminologists point out that young people have engaged in antisocial and criminal behaviour throughout history and their elders have always been 'outraged'. These 'moral panics' about youth criminality, they argue, may not accurately reflect reality.

Victims of violent crime

As well as carrying out the largest number of violent crimes, young, low-income, inner-city men are also the most common victims of theft, assault and other forms of violence. When young men are members of minority groups they are even more likely to be targeted. This is because minority

weblinks

For more information on violent crime, and who commits it, go to www.waylinks.co.uk/series/21debates/violence

A Gay Pride march in Brighton, UK, 1995. Although society is generally more tolerant of homosexuality than it used to be, many homosexuals still find themselves subjected to verbal abuse and violence.

groups, whether defined by race, gender, sexuality or class, tend to be viewed as a threat to society. Homosexuals, for example, experience a high incidence of violent crime and harassment.

Turning to crime

Why are young men from deprived backgrounds so much more likely than young girls from similar backgrounds to be involved in serious crimes? There are several possible reasons. One is that, from an early age, boys may join gangs in which crime is a way of life. Gangs can provide companionship, excitement and a sense of belonging. Once gang members are labelled as criminals by the authorities, it is easy to continue down 'the path of crime'.

Another factor may be the rapidly changing position of men in society. In previous generations, young men could look forward to getting a job and taking on the role of father and breadwinner in the family. However, changes in the labour market have made unemployment and job insecurity a real threat. Meanwhile, women are growing increasingly independent, both financially and emotionally. These changes in social and family structures have challenged traditional ideas about masculinity. Having a job is perhaps the most important legitimate way to gain respect in society. For a young man who has experienced a troubled, loveless childhood, the ability to earn a living can provide a sense of structure and stability in adulthood. Without this, some will perhaps find other, more destructive ways of establishing a position in society for themselves.

VIEWPOINT

'Young men at the margins of society are particularly prone to violent fights and these mostly occur on the streets round where [they] live and also around bars and other places selling alcohol.'
John Archer [ed.], Male Violence, *1995*

A group of youths on the street in a small English town. Boredom and frustration can lead some young people into vandalism and petty crime.

Violence and drugs

Illegal drugs are blamed for much of the increase in violent crime throughout the world. An illegal drug habit is expensive and addicts may use violence to get the money they need to buy regular supplies. Some drugs increase the chances of violence occurring because they make people feel less inhibited. But many commentators argue that most of the violence associated with illegal drugs is really caused by the fact that the drugs are illegal. In 2002 the global drug trade was estimated to be worth up to US$500 billion a year. This multi-billion-dollar trade is controlled by organized gangs who engage in violent wars with each other to gain their share of the market. This keeps the price on the streets high and encourages people to risk their lives for profit.

As enforcement agencies begin to recognize that they are not winning 'the war against drugs', critics of current drug policies suggest decriminalizing some so-called soft drugs such as cannabis. Others suggest a more radical approach. They argue that the most effective way to prevent the violence associated with the use of illegal drugs would be to start treating drugs as a social and health issue (rather than a

VIEWPOINT

'It does increasingly seem to be the view, particularly of the police, that prohibition is ineffective. It is wasteful of police time and alienates police and citizens so that in many western societies they feel like an occupying army. It leaves control of the drug to the underworld and makes it difficult to carry out effective drug education.'
John Marks, Drugs Forum Trust, New Zealand, on legalizing cannabis

Almost all the world's coca plants and opium poppies, used to produce cocaine and heroin, are grown in developing countries such as Colombia. Here, members of a Colombian gang are involved in drug-related violence.

criminal problem) and provide treatment for those who are addicted to them. Prices would fall and the Colombian drug barons and inner-city street gangs would go out of business.

Guns and gun control

In April 2002, a German student injured and killed some twenty-four people at his college with several guns which he was licensed to have. He then killed himself. This shooting joined a growing list of multiple shootings that have horrified people everywhere. The killers are usually young males with grievances against society, school or classmates. Most normal young people sometimes experience feelings of anger and resentment, but, when those young people have easy access to guns, such feelings can create a lethal combination.

Students from Columbine High School, Colorado, USA, wait for their friends to escape the building where two of their fellow students opened fire, killing fifteen people, and injuring twenty-three more, before taking their own lives, in April 1999.

Despite passing some limited legislation to reduce the use of handguns, the US continues to have the highest gun ownership and correspondingly the highest annual number of gun deaths. Although adult murders have decreased since the mid-1990s, there has been a 58 per cent increase in gun deaths of under seventeen-year-olds since the early 1980s.

FACT

In the US more family members are killed by one of their own family's guns – by accident, suicide or an impulsive family quarrel – than are killed or even threatened by a criminal's gun.

While many people describe the increase in gun deaths as 'an epidemic', members of the pro-gun lobby – insisting that the American Constitution grants them the right to 'bear arms' in order to protect themselves – resist changes to the gun laws. Other countries, concerned at the increase in both legal and illegal gun sales, have introduced tougher gun controls. In 1997 handgun ownership was banned in the UK. However the ban only appears to affect law-abiding citizens. In 1997, handguns were used in 2,648 crimes, but by 2001 there was a 40 per cent increase to 3,685.

Two American boys fight over a gun they have found in their father's bedroom.

weblinks

For more information on organized crime go to www.waylinks.co.uk/series/ 21debates/violence

Organized crime

Organized crime is a group enterprise that resembles a normal business but engages in illegal activities. Organized crime traditionally includes prostitution, smuggling (of drugs, goods and people), illegal gambling, large-scale theft, blackmail and intimidation. As members of these groups rely on absolute secrecy within their organization, threats, violence and bribes are commonly used to maintain discipline and loyalty.

Organized crime has become a multi-million-dollar business in the US, where it rivals the car industry in size. This type of crime has also become more sophisticated in its operation. In Britain some criminal organizations have found ways of laundering 'dirty money' (the proceeds of crime) by paying it into big clearing banks. They then withdraw 'clean money' and use it to set up legitimate businesses.

A masked, armed policeman leads away a Moscow businessman suspected of belonging to the Russian mafia.

Nearly every country has experience of organized crime. There are Japanese yakuza, Chinese triads, Sicilian mafia, and most recently the Russian mafia which some commentators believe is the most dangerous organization of all. Now, using computers and the Internet, these organizations have become less territorial. They operate within flexible international networks, forming alliances between groups involved in different illegal trades such as weapons trafficking and the sale of nuclear materials.

Corporate crime

Corporate crimes are offences committed by large companies and corporations. These increasingly powerful corporations touch our lives in many ways. They produce the food we eat, the drugs that combat our diseases, and the transport we use. When these products or services cause injury or death, it is often extremely difficult to identify the individual responsible so the whole company has to take responsibility.

VIEWPOINTS

'If the person accosted by a criminal is likely to be armed, if the home owners are presumed to have guns, most criminals will think twice before mugging, raping or burglarizing .... you can't defend yourself with a gun control law.'
From USA Today, 1993

'Statistics show that you are much more likely to be killed [in the US] if you are carrying a gun than if you are not.'
James Gilligan, Preventing Violence, 2001

FACT

In Austria, in 2002, sixteen officials appeared before a Salzburg court charged with causing the mountain train inferno which killed 155 people in the tunnel leading to Kaprun on the Kitzsteinhorn glacier in November 2000. The train company admitted that there was no emergency plan in the event of a fire, and no fire extinguishers or hammers in place.

Corporate crimes may seem less obviously violent than crimes commited by individuals (like assault or murder), but they are often further-reaching in their consequences. For example, American car manufacturers believed their cars would not sell as well if they were fitted with safety belts and so delayed their installation for decades, despite the evidence that safety belts would save thousands of lives. Likewise, British firms continued to expose their workers to asbestos long after its role in causing asbestosis (a fatal lung disease) had become known. All over the world, deaths from hazards at work far outnumber murders. Many of these deaths occur because firms ignore health and safety regulations.

Fears of violent crime

Whatever the facts, most people now believe that crime is more common and more serious. Surveys show that people are becoming more anxious about their homes being burgled and about being violently attacked. Women who have never been raped may be almost as fearful as those who have. They are often afraid of going out at night alone and equally afraid of staying on their own at home. Many elderly people are confined to their homes, frightened to open the door to anybody.

FACT

Although Japan and some US states are the only democracies to retain the death penalty, Japan has a relatively low crime rate, while the US has the highest murder rate in the developed world.

The fact that serious crimes are widely reported in the media probably contributes to this perception of a worldwide 'crime epidemic'. There is also a belief that the police are less effective in preventing and detecting crimes. Unfortunately, one of the results of these fears is that more people, particularly young men, are carrying guns and knives for protection. This actually increases the chances of serious injury or death. For example, in a confrontational situation, with one or all of the participants possibly under the influence of drugs or alcohol, it is all too easy to pull out a knife or a gun.

Crime and punishment

When people break the law, they are arrested and charged by the police, and judged and punished by the courts. Most violent criminals are given a prison sentence. The more dangerous the individual is considered to be, the longer the sentence. Prisons are supposed to punish criminals and also rehabilitate them (prepare them to return as honest members of society). Long prison sentences are thought to deter people from committing crimes but their success is debatable. The US, which has one of the world's harshest justice systems, also has, proportionately, the highest crime rates in the developed world.

DEBATE

As prisons do not seem to prevent crime and do not appear to adequately rehabilitate prisoners to face the outside world, what alternatives would you suggest and why?

Death row inmate Genaro Comacho Junior, in prison in Texas, USA. He was executed on 26 August 1998 by lethal injection.

RACISM
AND VIOLENCE

───── **weblinks** ─────

For more information
about living with racism go to
www.waylinks.co.uk/series/
21debates/violence

An Australian Aboriginal couple.
After the British arrived in Australia in
1788, many of the native Aborigines
were killed and their land was seized.
Since the Native Title Act was passed
in 1994, Aborigines have been able to
reclaim some of their land but they still
experience racism and are
discriminated against in health,
education, employment and housing.

What is racism?

Racism means treating people in a hostile or oppressive way because they belong to a different ethnic group. Such prejudice usually produces fear and antagonism between groups, and can easily spill over into violence. For millions of people, in many countries, racial violence is a real threat in their everyday lives. It may take the form of name-calling, harassment and abuse, and it sometimes leads to vicious racist attacks and murders. Racism often results in people of different ethnic origins being deprived of decent education, housing and jobs.

Theories of race

Prejudice and discrimination have existed throughout human history. However modern racism seems to have risen out of the exploitative relationship that Europeans established with non-white people in the eighteenth century. The slave trade could not have flourished without the widespread European belief that blacks belonged to an inferior race. Racism also helped to justify colonial rule over non-white peoples in such countries as Australia, New Zealand and Africa during the eighteenth and nineteenth centuries.

Count Joseph de Gobineau (1816-1882), sometimes called 'the father of modern racism', proposed that white people possessed superior intelligence, morality and willpower. These ideas influenced Adolf Hitler who transformed them into the ideology of the Nazi Party in Germany, which was responsible for the murder of millions of Jews and Gypsies during the 1930s and 1940s.

Since the Second World War, 'race science' has been thoroughly discredited. Experts now agree that there are no clear-cut biological differences between races, only a range of physical variations in human beings. Nevertheless white supremacist groups, such as the Ku Klux Klan and the Aryan Nations groups in the US, and Neo-Nazi groups in Europe, still firmly believe in the idea of racial superiority.

Ku Klux Klan members on the march in Houston, Texas, USA, in 2000, when an African-American, Gary Graham, was scheduled to be executed for the 1981 shooting of a white man.

The rise of fascist political groups

Individuals or gangs of youths expressing the racist attitudes of their families or local communities commit many of the attacks on ethnic minority groups in the UK and Europe. It is estimated that there are over 130,000 racially motivated crimes a year in the UK. People from ethnic minorities are much more likely than white people to be the targets of an attack.

VIEWPOINT

'Human beings tend to fear, or at least feel cautious towards, anything or anyone very new or different. This may be natural, but it doesn't mean it's good or that human beings can't progress beyond these rather primitive emotions.'
British Humanist Association

VIEWPOINT

'Firms don't give me a chance to prove I can do the job. At least 20 per cent of it is being black. I know I can do the job.'
Michael Oyeniyi, unemployed computer technician, UK, 2000

Smoke rises from burning vehicles during rioting in Bradford, in the north of England, in July 2001. About 200 police faced thousands of Asian youths who threw petrol bombs, bricks and bottles in clashes triggered by far-right white supremacists' plans to hold a rally in the town.

The rise of extreme right-wing or fascist political groups, with their belief in the superiority of the white race, has alarmed many people. These far-right organizations believe that violence should be used against those they hate. They exploited the downturn in the European economies in the 1990s by encouraging those fearful for their jobs and quality of life to blame 'foreigners' for unemployment and other social problems. In Germany, there were thousands of attacks on people the Neo-Nazis considered to be immigrants. For example, in 1992, ten-year-old Yeliz Arslan was killed in a firebomb attack on her house with other members of her family. Of Turkish origin, she had been born in Germany where her parents had lived for twenty-three years. Most Germans were appalled and many marched in silent protest.

In 2002, Jean-Marie Le Pen, leader of the extreme right French National Front, reached the final stages of the election for President. The French public, alarmed at this turn of events, voted in larger numbers than expected to block his election. In the UK, the British National Party (BNP) has had limited success in local elections, and Neo-Nazi groups have been implicated in some inner-city racial riots.

Institutional racism

Some commentators argue that racism does not only exist among small groups of individuals. They suggest that racism is present throughout society's structures and institutions, including schools,

the police and the health service. They claim that these organizations promote policies that favour certain groups while discriminating against others. For example, in 1993, a black teenager, Stephen Lawrence, was killed by five white youths in South London. The fact that no one has been convicted of his murder has been seen as evidence of racism in the British police and criminal justice system. The shooting of Amadou Diallo in New York, in 1999, raised similar concerns in the US. Believing that Diallo, a Guinean immigrant, had a gun, the police shot him forty-three times. The police authorities were strongly criticized for backing tough 'law and order' policies that disproportionately targeted non-white New Yorkers.

Neville and Doreen Lawrence, Stephen Lawrence's parents. A 1998 government inquiry found that the police had failed to provide an adequate service in the hunt for Stephen's killers because the Lawrences were black.

weblinks

For more information on the history of racism and issues of equality go to **www.waylinks.co.uk/series/ 21debates/violence**

Ethnic conflict

All over the world, people come into regular contact with other people who look different, and perhaps also think and live differently. Some welcome this ethnic mix, while others find it dangerous and threatening. When there is competition for resources, employment and housing, differences in language, religion and culture may become exaggerated. In this situation, there can be suspicion, tension and sometimes violence between the different ethnic groups.

Conflicts in the former Yugoslavia have involved attempts at 'ethnic cleansing' (the forced movement of ethnic groups, usually using violence, threats and harassment). The war in Kosovo in 1999 was prompted by charges that Serbians were ethnically cleansing the Kosovar Albanian (Muslim) population from the province.

Genocide

The term 'genocide' refers to the systematic elimination of one ethnic group by another.

Children passing Kosovar Albanian houses destroyed by Serbs during 'ethnic cleansing' in 1999.

The twentieth century has seen the emergence of 'organized genocide', with the Nazi Holocaust being the most horrific example of planned extermination. In 1994, the ethnic Hutu majority in Rwanda launched a genocidal campaign against the ethnic Tutsi minority. Some 800,000 people were killed within three months, and 2 million refugees spilled over into Burundi and Zaire (now the Democratic Republic of the Congo).

Seeking asylum

In 2000, around 150 million migrants were living outside their countries of birth. Of these, some 50 million people had been forced to flee their homes as a result of ethnic violence, racism and racial discrimination. Most refugees either move within their own country or into neighbouring states, hoping to return to their homes once there is peace. Some, who fear imprisonment or persecution for racial or political reasons, seek asylum in other countries. Those who suffer from poverty (often known as 'economic migrants') migrate to find a better life for their families.

Many industrialized, developed states, fearful of being overwhelmed by different ethnic groups, have introduced tighter immigration controls. Negative and inaccurate portrayals of asylum seekers and refugees in the media, and comments by politicians and public officials, have contributed to the climate of hostility towards these groups. There has been an alarming rise in racist violence in Sweden, the UK and Australia, including gang rape of refugee women.

Meanwhile, some asylum seekers and migrants, desperate to enter developed countries, pay large sums of money to smuggling syndicates who offer to help them avoid border controls. These arrangements are often extremely dangerous and can lead to tragedy.

VIEWPOINTS

'The overall picture that emerges from the recent press coverage is that asylum seekers are here [in the UK] to cheat us and take away from society.'
Tony Kushner and Katherine Knox, Refugees in an Age of Genocide, 1999

'Foreigners put 10 per cent more into the system than they take out.'
Home Office, UK, 2001

weblinks

For more information on refugees and asylum seekers go to
www.waylinks.co.uk/series/21debates/violence

DEBATE

Many countries now consider themselves 'multicultural'. How can the governments of such countries include ethnic minority groups and reduce racism? How do the cultures of different ethnic groups enrich communities?

POLITICAL VIOLENCE

Demonstrations and riots

In democracies, individuals can vote for the government they want. But, even in a democracy, people sometimes wish to protest about government policies or support particular causes. In countries where people have basic rights of free expression, anyone can join in a peaceful protest, march or meeting. But some people believe that the only way to attract attention for a cause is to use violence.

The demonstration then becomes a riot. Through the centuries, people have demonstrated and rioted for a variety of political reasons, including unfair taxes, environmental concerns, land reforms, political and racial discrimination, and oppressive government policies.

Gagged (to represent their loss of freedom), Tibetan women exiles staged a silent protest in 1995, in Huairou, China, against the Chinese occupation of their country.

weblinks

For more information on state violence go to
www.waylinks.co.uk/series/
21debates/violence

Revolutions and invasions

Occasionally entire groups of people become so disillusioned by their country's political system that they deliberately use violence to overthrow an existing government. The French Revolution of 1789 and the Russian Revolution of 1917, both very bloody affairs, were extreme political protests. By comparison the 'velvet revolutions', the overthrow of the communist systems in Eastern Europe and the former USSR from 1989, while no less dramatic, were much less violent. Revolutions attract great attention but in fact occur relatively rarely.

Larger nations sometimes invade their more vulnerable neighbours and deprive them of their independence. In 1975, Indonesia annexed (took control of) East Timor. Protest movements in East Timor sought to achieve both independence and democracy. Many activists were imprisoned, tortured or executed by their oppressors. In 1999, an Indonesian student-led demonstration forced President Suharto to resign. Several months later, the East Timorese voted overwhelmingly for independence from Indonesia. In 2001 democratic elections were held and the Independence Party (Fretlin), which had led the 24-year-long struggle for independence, was voted in.

Protesters hurl stones at Indonesian anti-riot police in Jakarta in 1998. Several students died in clashes with the security forces during the unrest.

Violence by the state

Increasingly, people around the world are demonstrating for their right to live in peace with a government of their choice. But authoritarian regimes may use violence against their own populations in order to keep power and wealth in the hands of a very small group. In 1989, for instance, thousands of protesting students were killed in China's Tiananmen Square when the government crushed their movement for democracy.

The powerful monarchies in Saudi Arabia and Kuwait also strictly limit their citizens' civil rights and deny them any real participation in government affairs. Those who challenge the system may be obliged to escape, and join the increasing number of political refugees seeking asylum in more democratic countries.

FACT

In May 2002, the military junta which holds power in Burma released the pro-democracy leader, Aung San Suu Kyi, from house arrest. In 1990 the junta allowed elections. The National League for Democracy, of which Aung San Suu Kyi was co-founder, won 82 per cent of the seats, but the junta refused to recognize the result and arrested all members of parliament. The junta is also accused of serious human rights abuses against their own people.

Terrorism

Terrorism usually refers to the deliberate killing of civilians in order to affect policies and laws. Terrorist acts of violence include bombings, hijackings, hostage-taking, assassinations, and threats against civilians. Although terrorism has existed throughout history it began to achieve particular prominence during the second half of the twentieth century, with the growth of extreme left-wing terrorist movements such as the Baader-Meinhof group in West Germany and the Red Brigades in Italy. A desire to set up separate states within states has motivated the terrorist activities of such groups as the Basque separatists in Spain, the Tamil Tigers in Sri Lanka, and the Chechen rebels in southern Russia. However it is the conflict between Israel and the Arab nations that has caused most of the international terrorist activity since the 1960s.

A woman is carried to an ambulance by emergency workers following a bombing by the militant Palestinian group HAMAS at Jerusalem's Hebrew University in July 2002. The blast killed at least seven people and wounded more than eighty others. Losses on both sides increase hatred and make it harder to find a solution to the conflict between the Palestinians and Israelis.

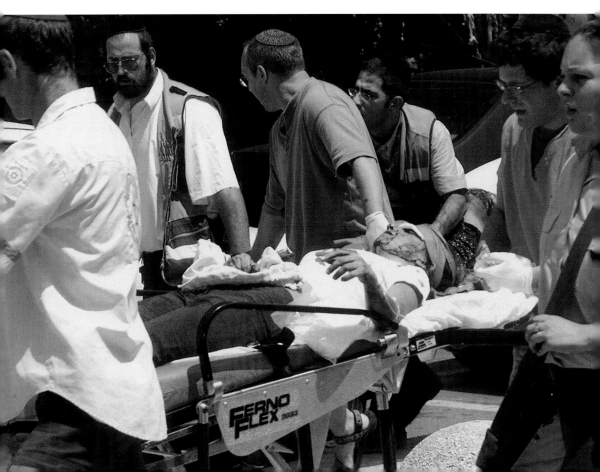

The rise of religious fundamentalism

As countries have modernized over the last two or three decades, some members of Christian and Islamic communities have become concerned about the undermining of many traditional values, including the importance of the family and a woman's so-called duty to obey her husband. Fundamentalism can be viewed as a return to traditional social values and religious beliefs.

In some sectors of the Islamic world this religious revival has been accompanied by a reaction against the impact of the developed world, particularly the USA. These sentiments are partly historical but they also spring from the USA's continuing support for Israel, and its military presence in Arab countries. This antagonism has been demonstrated over the years by a number of terrorist incidents culminating in the destruction of New York's World Trade Center in New York, which killed over three thousand people of all nationalities, and the attack on the Pentagon in Virginia, on 11 September 2001. Al-Qaida, a loose network of terrorists headed by Osama Bin Laden, was considered responsible for what was viewed by all faiths and nationalities as a barbaric act against humanity.

The US has seen the largest growth in Christian fundamentalist movements, a few of which have been associated with violence. Perhaps the best-known example is the People's Temple. Their leader, Jim Jones, took about a thousand of his followers from California to establish a religious community in Guyana, South America. After a visiting US Congressman was murdered, Jim Jones is said to have ordered his followers to commit suicide. Over 900 men, women and children died.

VIEWPOINT

'People who have been dispossessed, degraded, humiliated, but whose spirit has not been broken, understandably want to proclaim their grievances, whether or not they expect the proclamation to advance their cause... The ones we call terrorists are the ones who have succeeded in that goal and used violence to succeed in it.'
Annette C. Baier. Violence. Terrorism and Justice. 1991

DEBATE

If we want the world to become less violent, is violent protest ever justifiable?

VIOLENCE AS ENTERTAINMENT

The appeal of violence

Many individuals enjoy watching violent entertainment as long as they, the spectators, are not at risk. For example, the Romans revelled in watching battles between slaves who were forced to fight each other to the death. In modern times, this fascination encourages the media to focus on violence, whether it is in the reporting of world news or stories about murderers and serial killers on television, film, video or in literature. Science fiction can also be extremely violent, with its depictions of alien creatures being destroyed or

Young children watching a violent TV programme.

waging war on humankind. In the light of all this, increasing concern is being expressed about the effects of seeing so much violence. A 1992 study by the American Psychological Association claimed that the average American child or teenager viewed 10,000 murders, rapes and assaults per year on television, with children's cartoons showing the highest number of violent acts. Research carried out over the last three decades suggests that watching screen violence for long periods of time may stimulate violent behaviour in some vulnerable children and young people.

There are three main concerns about the effects of viewing violence. Firstly, people could develop favourable attitudes towards violence because violent acts may be seen as an acceptable response to stress or anger. Secondly, by depicting violence as entertainment, rather than as tragedy, these films or computer games could make viewers less sensitive to violence and the effects on its victims. Thirdly, watching a lot of violence may encourage the belief that the world is as nasty and dangerous in real life as it is in television programmes.

Reporting the news

The media also reports on real-life events around the world. This may involve showing violence but its effects on the viewer are very different from the effects of watching a violent film or drama. Television broadcasters in particular accept that they have a duty to educate, to provide information about events, so that people can gain an understanding of the issues involved. For instance, wars – such as those in Afghanistan and Iraq – have had extensive television coverage. But watching real violence being inflicted on other people, seeing the wreckage of homes and villages, horrifies many and may encourage people to find other ways to resolve conflicts.

VIEWPOINTS

'There have been allegations that Oliver Stone's movie, *Natural Born Killers* has inspired up to ten "copy" killings. In Dallas, a 14-year-old boy decapitated [beheaded] a young girl after seeing the film and told friends he wanted to be famous like "the natural born killers" in the movie.'
Guardian *newspaper, UK*

'It is as silly to blame a single film as it is to indict [accuse] the Bible which forensic researchers have found to be the single most frequently quoted justification used by "noble-cause" killers who murder prostitutes and homosexuals.'
Guardian *newspaper, UK*

DEBATE

Do you think being a spectator of violence influences violent behaviour in any way? If we believe we are a civilized society, should we still be entertained by violence?

Censorship

Many countries use rating systems with age restrictions or recommendations for admission to films that may contain violence. Because young people can get access to videos relatively easily, these are even more carefully censored; sometimes more extreme scenes are cut entirely. In the UK, television material considered unsuitable for children is shown later in the evening.

With the rise of the Internet it has become more difficult to control what people see. Many people think that violence and psychological horror should be limited in films aimed at the younger age group but that there should be a more relaxed attitude to sex, nudity and drugs. Anti-censorship campaigners suggest a system which gives a rough guide to the content of entertainment material and allow parents to decide what their children watch.

Ice hockey is popular in the US but can be a violent game. Here, a brawl breaks out on the ice after a Syracuse crunch goal during a home game against the Kentucky Thoroughblades.

Violence in sport

Team sports often involve violence – whether it is a rugby player's tackle or a hockey stick that connects with a shin. Tension runs high, and tempers get frayed when there is foul play or good results fail to materialize. Many critics fear that, in professional sport, violence is now becoming part of the game. In spite of condemnation by both players and the public, violent behaviour is often tolerated. The media also plays a part: while appearing to condemn violent acts, it frequently pays considerable attention to them.

In some sports, such as football, huge amounts of money are paid to top footballers who attract

large crowds and earn their clubs big rewards.
While clubs and managers may express dismay at
violent behaviour they are often reluctant to
reprimand such players.

There is also the problem of violence among fans.
Most football fans at a match will express some
friendly rivalry, but this can sometimes spill over
into violence. It has been suggested that Britain
invented football, and, sometime later,
hooliganism. In fact other football nations, such as
Brazil and Argentina as well as some European
countries, all have their own brands of
hooliganism, including street fighting, vandalism
and drunkenness. In 1985, the behaviour of a
number of British football fans led to the deaths of
thirty-eight people, most of them Italian, at the
Heysel Stadium in Belgium. As a punishment,
English football clubs were banned for several years
from playing in Europe.

*A group of British football fans
clash with local French youths in
Marseilles, after England defeated
Tunisia 2-0, in 1998.*

VIEWPOINT

'The main concern over boxing is the brain damage ... most signs of brain damage are more likely to appear towards the end of a boxer's career.'
British Medical Association

With better co-operation between police, football bodies and fans, football violence has been significantly reduced since the 1980s. Known troublemakers have their passports removed, rival fans are usually separated at matches, and alcohol is banned or discouraged.

Mike Tyson bites Evander Holyfield's ear during the WBA Heavyweight Championship fight in Las Vegas, USA, in 1997. Tyson was disqualified.

However, in some sports, such as boxing and wrestling, violence is the central aim. Boxers and wrestlers both try to injure each other, and a considerable number of boxers have been permanently injured or killed as a result of their fights. There have been calls for boxing to be banned, as it is in Sweden. However defenders of the sport suggest that this would simply drive it underground where it would be impossible to monitor. They also point out that people choose to box; they are not forced to do so.

FACT

In 2002, eight years after Oregon voters had outlawed bear hunting with hounds, poachers were still a major threat to the American black bear. According to the poachers, it was well worth breaking the law when a single bear's gallbladder, used for medicinal purposes in South-East Asian countries, could fetch $400.

Killing for sport

Violence towards animals arouses a wide range of bitterly opposed opinions, especially – in the UK – when it comes to hunting. Some people argue that hunting foxes, deer, hares and other animals for sport is the best way of keeping their numbers down. They suggest that the animal does not suffer either during the chase or the kill. Others claim that hunting is cruel and mainly carried out for the pleasure of the hunters. Anti-hunt demonstrators have staged many peaceful protests but there have also been cases of violence and personal attacks on hunters, to get their message across. This condemnation of killing for sport is a relatively recent phenomenon as people have become more aware of the number of animal species that are now threatened or endangered. For example, during the nineteenth century sportsmen from many countries went to India to hunt tigers. Now the tiger is one of the main examples of an animal needing protection from human killers.

Other forms of violence against animals cause even more outrage. Dog fighting and cock fighting, for instance, are banned in many countries, yet both continue to flourish illegally. People bet on dogs or cockerels that are made to fight until one is dead or too badly injured to continue. Poaching is another form of cruelty towards animals, often driven by the thriving trade in animal parts used in traditional Chinese medicine.

VIEWPOINTS

'So far, all our financial and human resources have had to go into defending hunting and this makes us appear very reactionary. In an ideal world, the currently hostile government would give us five years in which to find out what changes would make hunting more acceptable to the wider public and then to implement them.'
Michael Sagar, Horse and Hounds magazine, UK, 2001

'People are abusing, tormenting and killing hares for the fun of it and this depravity should have no place in the Britain of 2001.'
Robert Jackson, MP, Observer newspaper, UK, 2001

Bullfighting, an ancient and violent Spanish custom, usually ends in death for the bull and can also be extremely dangerous for the bullfighter. Here, Jose Luis Parada bleeds after being gored during the traditional April bullfighting fair in Seville in 1995.

PREVENTING
VIOLENCE

Keeping the peace

At the end of the Second World War, there was a determination that the devastation of two world wars must never happen again, and the United Nations (UN) Organization was established to work for peace and international co-operation. The UN includes the United Nations Children's Fund (UNICEF) which works to protect children and young people from violence and abuse all over the world.

Many national governments, along with the UN and other international bodies such as the International Criminal Court in the Hague, are trying to find ways of ending collective violence in all its forms, including genocide, war crimes, racial discrimination and ethnic cleansing. For example, in 1996 the South African government set up the Truth and Reconciliation Commission to examine the abuses which had occurred under apartheid. The hearings were not intended to be trials, to apportion blame, but rather to acknowledge the injustices in an atmosphere of humility and open debate.

The world's wealthier nations are also starting to recognize that poverty and violence are interlinked, and that they have an obligation to reduce poverty and increase economic opportunities in the poorest nations. In 2002, the US and the European Union provided debt relief for twenty-four of the world's poorest countries but only on the condition that they put all the money into healthcare, education and development.

Starting from the beginning

People can 'learn' to be violent if they experience violence at a young age. Children who regard being hit as normal are more likely to bully and use violence in later life. In 1989 a major campaign was launched in the UK to help organizations all over the world to end all physical punishment of children. This includes not only 'smacking' but also the more extreme forms of violence such as beating and capital punishment. In 2000, a UK charity, the National Society for the Prevention of Cruelty to Children (NSPCC), set up the 'Full Stop' campaign which aims to eliminate child abuse by 2020. The NSPCC tries to prevent abuse occurring in the first place by encouraging all members of the community to take some responsibility for reporting it. In cases where children and young people have been abused, the NSPCC provides therapy to help them recover, making it less likely that they will abuse their own children.

A Brazilian boy learns to use the Internet at a school run by a non-profit organization in a shanty town in Rio de Janeiro, in 2001. The mothers of the poorest families are paid to send their children to school, in order to achieve greater economic equality and a more stable, peaceful society.

VIEWPOINT

'The only way to get kids not to hurt each other is to get kids not to want to hurt each other.'
Adrian LeBlanc, 'The Outsiders', New York Times Magazine

weblinks

For more information
on developing a less
violent world go to
www.waylinks.co.uk/series/
21debates/violence

As poverty is being recognized as a factor causing increased abuse and violence in families and communities, governments need to set up programmes that give poorer families financial and social support. Pre-school educational and family support programmes, such as Sure Start in the UK, have been shown to reduce later delinquency (law-breaking) and crime. Once children are at school, programmes teaching them how to resolve conflicts peacefully also appear to reduce the rate of future violence.

For several years, police in Boston, USA, have successfully applied a community policing and prevention approach to criminality in youth gangs. While stating very clearly that they would crack down firmly on all crime, they have also offered

A peace and reconciliation class supported by UNICEF in Burundi, 1995.

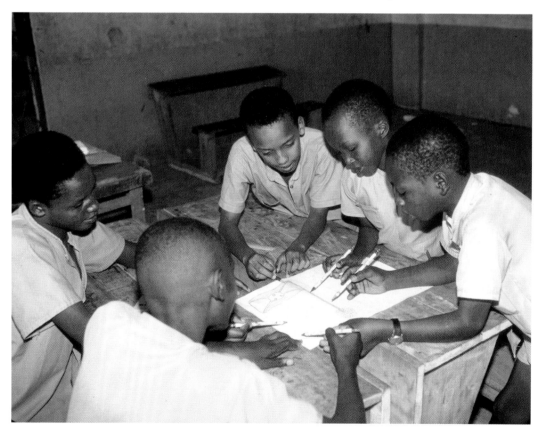

rehabilitation programmes for alcohol and drug addicts, and further education. Making education and employment accessible is one of the most effective and successful means of preventing violence.

What can you do?

Societies can only become less violent if we all recognize that it is possible to live our lives in a non-violent way. Some experts put this more forcefully: unless the human race takes steps to prevent violence, we may not survive this century.

- **How you and your friends live your lives can make a difference.**
  Home should be a safe place. If you know of anyone who is experiencing violence or abuse at home tell someone in authority that you trust – a parent or teacher. Do not agree to keep it a secret; abusers count on secrecy.

- **Schools should encourage non-violent attitudes.**
  If others are being hurt by bullies, don't stand by and let it happen. If you are putting yourself at risk then get assistance. Tell the victim that you want to help and encourage friends and classmates to do the same. Find out about your school's anti-bullying policy. Is it an effective policy or do you and your friends know of other non-violent procedures that you think would reduce bullying? Tell other young people about these.

There are many organizations that work to prevent violence (see Useful Addresses). You might like to join a local group, or organize a fundraising event. Remember, your voice counts. There is a Chinese proverb that says, 'A journey of a thousand miles begins with a single step.' If each of us takes a step to change attitudes and practices, the world will become a safer and happier place.

FACT

After nineteen years of violence, which left some 64,000 people dead, the rival sides in Sri Lanka returned to the negotiating table. In February 2002, the Tamil Tigers signed a ceasefire with the Sri Lankan government and agreed to meet for peace talks mediated by Norway.

DEBATE

Is it possible to have a non-violent world?

GLOSSARY

adultery sexual relations between a married person and someone other than their husband or wife.

annex (of a country or state) to take control of (another country or state).

apartheid meaning 'apartness'. A system of government introduced in South Africa in 1948 to keep black, white, mixed-race and Asian people separate and unequal.

assault to attack violently; a violent attack.

asylum seeker someone who suffers because of his or her skin colour, culture, religion or political beliefs, and flees to another country to seek asylum (a safe haven). Asylum also means the right to live in another country if you have been attacked for one of these reasons.

authoritarian demanding that rules and laws must always be obeyed whether or not they are right.

capital punishment punishment by death, according to law; execution; the death penalty.

censor to examine (films, videos, books, etc) and remove anything considered to be offensive.

Child Protection Register a list kept by UK social services departments of children and young people who have been identified as suffering significant harm.

civil war a war between citizens of the same country.

coercion persuading by force.

colonial rule control over people or areas; historically used by European countries, such as Britain, France, Spain and Portugal, to dominate countries in Africa, Asia and South America.

corporal punishment physical punishment, e.g. hitting or smacking.

courier (in the drugs trade) someone who carries illegal drugs from one country to another.

criminologist someone who studies criminal behaviour.

delinquency behaviour, especially by young people, that goes against accepted social standards or breaks the law.

democracy a political system in which citizens elect their own rulers and take part in decision-making.

deprived without food, money or comfortable living conditions.

developed countries the wealthier countries of the world, including those of Europe, North America, Japan and Australia and New Zealand. People living there are normally healthy, well educated and work in a wide variety of high-technology industries.

developing countries the poorer countries of the world, sometimes called the Third World and including much of Africa, Asia, Latin America and Oceania. People living there are often unhealthy, poorly educated and work in agriculture and lower-technology industries.

domestic violence term used to describe violence within a family setting, usually between adults.

dowry money or goods traditionally given by a bride's family to the bridegroom on marriage. Most commonly practised in India, it is now illegal there but the custom continues.

economy the system by which a country's wealth is produced and used.

ethnic cleansing the policy of forcing the people of a particular ethnic group or religion to leave an area or country.

ethnic group a group of people who share a common culture, tradition and sometimes language.

fascist someone who obeys one powerful leader, opposes democracy, and believes that their country or ethnic group is better than all others.

fundamentalism the practice of following the traditional rules of a religion, such as Christianity or Islam, very exactly.

gender the division into male or female.

genocide the deliberate killing of a people or nation.

globalization growing social and economic interdependence between different peoples and countries in the world.

harassment repeated verbal or physical attacks.

heterosexual someone who is sexually attracted to people of the opposite sex.

homicide murder.

homosexual someone who is sexually attracted to people of the same sex.

hooliganism noisy, rough, aggressive behaviour, sometimes associated with football spectators.

Hutterite member of the Anabaptist sect who came from Eastern Europe during the nineteenth century to escape religious persecution.

ideology a set of ideas, especially one on which a political or economic system is based.

International Labour Organization (ILO) a UN organization which investigates working conditions around the world and proposes legislation to protect workers from abuse and hazards in the workplace.

intimidate to bully, threaten or frighten.

junta a government (especially a military one) that has come to power by force rather than through elections.

masculinity qualities traditionally considered typical of a man, e.g. strength, self-reliance and the ability to support a family.

minority group a group of people in a society who are set apart from the majority population by their physical or cultural differences. Minority groups often experience hostility and unfair treatment.

National Society for the Prevention of Cruelty to Children (NSPCC) a UK charity that is concerned with children's welfare.

paedophile an adult who seeks to have sex with children.

perpetrator someone who does something wrong or criminal.

post traumatic stress disorder a condition of mental stress, anxiety, and sometimes physical illness which may follow injury or psychological shock.

rape to have sex with someone against their will.

refugee someone who has been forced to leave their country for political reasons or during a war.

rehabilitate to help someone find ways of fitting in to society (e.g. when coming out of prison), through education, retraining, new employment, or therapy.

syndicate a group of people or companies combined together for a particular purpose, usually business.

therapy treatment of physical or mental disorders without using drugs or surgery.

zero tolerance policing an approach to crime prevention that emphasizes maintaining order by targeting small-scale crime and minor disturbances in order to prevent more major crime problems.

BOOKS TO READ

FICTION
Breadwinner
Deborah Ellis
(Oxford University Press, 2001)

Girl in Red
Gaye Hicyilmaz
(Orion, 2000)

Jake's Tower
Elizabeth Laird
(Macmillan, 2002)

Junk
Melvyn Burgess
(Puffin, 1997)

Noughts and Crosses
Malorie Blackman
(Corgi, 2002)

NON-FICTION
Talking Points: Genocide
Reg Grant
(Hodder Wayland, 1998)

New Perspectives: Israel and Arab Nations in Conflict
Nathaniel Harris
(Hodder Wayland, 1998)

Refugees and Asylum Seekers (Issues Series)
Craig Donellan (ed.)
(Independence Educational Publishers, 1999)

USEFUL ADDRESSES

Amnesty International
99-119 Roseberry Avenue
London EC1R 4RE
Tel: 0207 814 6200

British Humanist Association
47 Theobald's Road
London WC1X 8SP
Tel: 0207 430 0908

Childline
2nd Floor
Royal Mail Building
Studd Street
London N1 OQW
Tel: 0207 239 1000

Commission for Racial Equality
Elliot House
10-12 Arlington Street
London SE1E 5EH
Tel: 0207 828 7022

NSPCC
National Centre
Curtain Road
London EC2A 3NH
Tel: 0207 825 2500

Refugee Council
3 Bondway
London SW8 1SJ
Tel: 0207 820 3000

Save the Children Fund
17 Grove Lane
Camberwell
London SE5 8RD
Tel: 0207 703 5400

UNICEF
Africa House
66-78 Kingsway
London WC2B 6NB
Tel: 0207 405 5592

INDEX

Numbers in **bold** refer to illustrations.

Aboriginal people **40**
abuse
    child 4, 11, 20, 22, 24, 25, **25**, 57, 59
    physical 9, 11, 12, 13, 14, 15, 16, 17, 18, 19, 20, 21, 22, 23,
        24, 57
    psychological 5, 9, 11, 20, 23
    racist 40, 41, **41**, 42, **42**, 43, **43**, 44, **44**, 45, 56
    sexual 4, 5, 11, 12, 14, 16, 20, 21, 22, 25, 26, 31, 45, 57
Afghanistan 6, **7**, 26, 51
Africa 15, 40
aggression 6, 23
alcohol 31, 38, 54, 59
al-Qaida 49
American Constitution 36
Angola 8, 26
animals, violence against 54, 55, **55**
apartheid 56
Argentina 53
Aryan Nations 41
Asia 15, 27
assault 11, 17, 30, 31, 32, 51
asylum seekers 45, 47
Australia 14, 40, **40**, 45

Bangladesh 29
Belgium 53
Bin Laden, Osama 49
blackmail 36
bombs 6, 7, **7**, 48, **48**
boxing 54, **54**
Brazil 16, 53, **57**
British National Party 42
Bulger, James 24
bullfighting **55**
bullying 9, 19, 23, 24, 57, 59
burglary 31, 38
Burkina Faso 28
Burundi 45, **58**

Cambodia **8**, **15**, **27**
Canada 9, 21
capital punishment 57, 39, **39**
care, children in 12, 13, 22
censorship 52
Chechnya 48
child abuse 4, 11, 20, 22, 24, 25, **25**, 57
child labour 28, **28**, 29, **29**
child protection 12, 13, 22
Child Protection Register 12
Children Act 12, 13
children and violence 4, 11, 16, **16**, 17, **17**, 18, 20,
    21, 23, 24, 25, **25**, 26, **26**, 27, **27**, 28, **28**, 29, **29**,
    50, 51, 52
China 11, **46**, 47
Christianity 49
civil war 6, **6**, 7, 45
cock fighting 55
Colombia 26, **34**, 35
colonialism 40
Columbine High School **35**
Convention on the Rights of the Child 22

corporal punishment 9, 11
crime 4, 5, 6, 23, 30, 31, 38, 58
    corporate 37, 38
    drug-related 34, **34**, 35
    organized 36, 37, **37**
    perpetrators of 6, 31, 32, 33, 39, **39**, 58
    and punishment 39, **39**
    victims of 32, **32**, 33

debt relief 56
democracy 46, 47
Democratic Republic of the Congo 8, 45
demonstrations 46, **46**, 55
developed countries 12, 14, 18, 22, 31, 39, 45, 49
developing countries 14, 15, 26, 28, 29
Diallo, Amadou 43
dog fighting 55
domestic violence 5, 9, 11, 12, 13, **13**, 14, 15, **15**, 16, 17, 18,
    19, 20, **20**, 21, 31
diseases 28, 38
dowry killings 15
drugs, illegal 27, 31, 34, **34**, 38, 59

East Timor 47
education 27, 29, 51, 56, **57**, 58, 59
Egypt **29**
elderly people, violence against 18, 19, **19**, 38
endangered species 55
ethnic conflict 44, **44**
Europe 14, 27, 41, 42, 46, 53, 56
execution **39**

families, violence in 5, 11, 12, 13, **13**, 14, 15, 15, 16, 17, 18, 19,
    20, **20**, 21, 22, 58, 59
fascism 41, 42
football 52, 53, **53**, 54
foster care 13
France 42, 46, **53**

gambling 36
gangs 33, 34, 35, 58
genetics and violence 6
genocide 44, 45, 56
Germany 35, 40, 42, 48
Gobineau, Count Joseph de 40
goldmining 28
guns 6, 35, **35**, 36, **36**, 38

health and safety regulations 38
Hitler, Adolf 40
Holocaust 45
Holyfield, Evander **54**
homelessness 22, 23, **23**
homosexuals and violence 19, **32**, 33
hooliganism 53, **53**
hunting 54, 55
Hutterites 9

ice hockey **52**
India 11, 15, 27, 28, 55
Indonesia 47, **47**
inequality 6
International Labour Organization 28, 29

INDEX

Internet 25, 37, 52, **57**
invasions, military 47
Iraq 15
Islam 49
Israel **20**, 48, **48**, 49
Italy 29, 48

Japan 6
Jones, Jim 49

knives 38
Kosovo 44, **44**, 51
Ku Klux Klan 41, **41**
Kuwait 47

labourers, child 28, **28**, 29, **29**
Latin America 27
Lawrence, Stephen 43, **43**
Le Pen, Jean-Marie 42
legal systems 9, 15, 16, 39, 43
legislation 12, 13, 14, 19, 22, 35, 36
Levinson, David 13
Liberia 8, **26**
Lombroso, Cesare 6

mafia 37, **37**
media, violence in the 4, 16, 24, 30, 32, 38, 50, **50**, 51, 52
men and violence 16, **16**, 17, **17**, 31, 32, **32**, 33, **33**
Menendez, Lyle and Erik 18
mental illness 20, 22
minority groups 32, **32**, 33, 40, 41, 42, 43
mobile phones 23, 31
morality 32
Mozambique 8, 26
murder 4, 9, 11, 14, 16, 18, **18**, 24, **25**, 30, 35, **35**, 43, **43**, 49, 51

National Front, French 42
Nazis 40, 45
Neo-Nazis 41, 42
New Zealand 14, 40
non-violent societies 9
Northern Ireland **5**
Norway 6
National Society for the Prevention of Cruelty to Children 11, 57

orphans **12**, 27
organized crime 36, 37, **37**

paedophiles 24, 25, **25**
Pakistan **28**
Palestinians 48, **48**
poaching 55
police 9, 14, 20, 25, 27, 31, 38, 39, 43, **47**, 54, 58
political violence **5**, 46, **46**, 47, **47**, 48, **48**, 49
post traumatic stress disorder 5, 20
poverty 6, 8, 9, **12**, 27, 28, 31, 33, 45, 56, 58
preventing violence 21, **21**, 24, 25, 34, 35, 36, 54, 56, 57, **57**, 58, **58**, 59
prisons 20, 39, **39**
prostitution 27, 31, 36
psychological problems 21, **21**, 24, 27, 33, 35, 51, 57
psychotherapy 20, 21, 57

racism 40, 41, **41**, 42, **42**, 43, **43**, 44, **44**, 45, 56
rape 4, 5, 14, 30, 31, 38, 51
refugees 6, **6**, 26, 45, 47
religious fundamentalism 49
revolutions 46
riots 42, **42**, 46, **47**
Russia 37, **37**, 46
Rwanda **6**, 45

Samoa 9
Saudi Arabia 47
Save the Children 26
Second World War 30, 40, 56
Serbia 44, **44**
shoplifting 31
slave trade 40
smacking 9, 57
smuggling 36, 45
social problems and violence 6, 9, 12, 16, 22, 23, 26, 27, 31, 33, 34, 42, 56, 58
soldiers, child 26, **26**, 27
South Africa 17, 56
Spain 48
sport, violence in 52, **52**, 53, **53**
Sri Lanka 48
street children 27
street fighting 53, **53**
Suharto, President 47
suicide 9, 24, 49
Sweden 6, 9, 45, 54

terrorism 48, **48**, 49
theft 31, 32, 36
Tibet **46**
triads 37
truancy 32
Turkey 26
Tyson, Mike **54**

Uganda 8
UK 9, 12, **12**, 14, 20, 24, 36, 37, 38, 41, 42, **42**, 43, 45, 52, 57, 58
unemployment 23, 33
United Nations 56
United Nations Children's Fund 29, 56, **58**
USA 9, **10**, 14, 18, 20, 35, **35**, 36, **36**, 37, 38, **39**, **41**, 43, 49, 52, 56, 58

vandalism 32, 53
Violence Against Women Act 14

war, violence in 5, 6, 7, **7**, 8, 9, 26, **26**, 27, **27**, 44, **44**, 45, 51, 56
weapons 6, **6**, **7**, 35, **35**, 36, **36**, 37, 38
white supremacists 41, 42
wife beating 13, 14, 16, 20, **20**
workplace bullying 9
women
   and crime 31
   violence against 11, 13, **13**, 14, 15, **15**, 16, 17, 19, 20, **20**, 30, 31, 38, 45
wrestling 54

yakuza 37
Yugoslavia, former 27, 44, **44**